"PYTHON CHRONICLES: ENCHANTED CODING QUESTS FOR YOUNG SORCERERS"

Contents

"Python Chronicles: Enchanted Coding Quests for Young Sorcerers"...1

Welcome to Python Wonderland: An Experiment for Young Programmers!...............3

    1. A Brief look into the Coding Wonderland ..3

    2. Meet Python, Your New Coding Buddy......4

2. Setting Up Your Coding Camp........................6

    2.1 Opening up Your Coding Apparatuses 6

    2.2 Creating Your Private Coding 7

3. Hi, World! Enchantment Spell......................10

    3.1 Projecting Your Most memorable Spell: print("Hello, World!") 10

    3.2 Figuring out the Enchanted behind the Spell 12

4. Journey into Variables 14

    4.1 Buying Magical Remedies: 14

    4.2 Blending Mixtures: Variable Task Stunts16

5. The Charmed Choice Woodland 18

    5.1 Exploring with if Explanations................18

5.2 Simply deciding: Elif and Other Adventures:.................................20

6. Circling through the Time Travel.................23

6.1 Dance of the For Circle............................23

6.2 Mission of the While Circle 25

7.Functions: Your Coding Spells Book..............28

7.1 Making Your Own Spells: Characterizing Capabilities....................................28

7.2 Projecting Spells Voluntarily: Calling Capabilities....................................31

8. Lists: The Enchanted Assortment.................34

8.1 Social event Antiques: Making Records .34

8.2 Sorting and Looking for Treasure...........36

9. Dictionaries: 39

9.1 Guide Making with Word references.....39

9.2 Gaining Access to Secrets: Getting to and Altering 41

10. The Excellent Finale: Smaller than usual Python Tasks 45

10.1 Planning Your Enchanted Elixir Blender 45

10.2 Structure Your Mythical serpent Tamer Game..48

4

11. Observing Your Coding Triumph 52

11.1 Your Python Experience Recognition ...52

11.2 Using Your Magical Skills Together:
Coding Exhibit 53

12. Appendix: The Alchemist's Tool
compartment 57

12.1 Spells for Quick Reference 1. Print Spell:
....57

12.2 Investigating Your Coding Cauldron 60

Welcome to Python Wonderland: An Experiment for Young Programmers!

Salutations, brave young coders!

Might it be said that you are prepared to set out on an exceptional excursion into the magical domain of coding? Prepare yourselves as we step into Python Wonderland, an enchanted spot where pieces and bytes dance, and coding spells show some major signs of life!

1. A Brief look into the Coding Wonderland

Envision an existence where you have the ability to make anything you can dream of, where your thoughts and creative mind are changed into lines of code that get things going. Welcome to the charming place that is known for Python, a language so cordial and flexible that it resembles having a mystical wand for coding undertakings.

2. Meet Python, Your New Coding Buddy

In this eccentric aide, you'll be acquainted with your new coding sidekick - Python, an enchanting and slithery language that is as simple to advance as doing magic. Together, we'll reveal the insider facts of Python and open the way to a reality where imagination exceeds all logical limitations.

However, before we jump into the coding wizardry, we should set up our coding camp and fabricate our mystery post. Prepare for an excursion loaded up with chuckling, disclosure, and the delight of transforming your most out of control thoughts into the real world.

2. Setting Up Your Coding Camp

2.1 Opening up Your Coding Apparatuses

Welcome, youthful coders, to the initial step of our fabulous experience! Similarly as each wizard needs their spellbook, and each knight their dependable blade, a coder needs their devices. We should open up the mystical coding devices that will enable you to make ponders in Python Wonderland.

The Wand: Your Reliable Computer
Take hold of your reliable device—your computer! Make sure it's prepared to channel the magic of Python, whether it's a spellbinding laptop or a mysterious desktop. Relax; no spells are finished without a PC close by!

The Remedies: Introducing Python
In our otherworldly land, Python is the language of decision. Get familiar with the spell to brew Python mixtures on your PC. We'll walk you through the delightful process of installing Python so you can start coding.

The Spellbook: Picking a Supervisor
Each wizard needs a spellbook, and each coder needs a code supervisor. Pick your spellbook astutely! We'll acquaint you with fledgling agreeable code editors that will turn into your reliable friends on this coding mission.

2.2 Creating Your Private Coding

Fortress Now that we have unwrapped our tools, it is time to construct a private coding fortress where fantasies can come true.

Picture it as your mysterious safe-haven, where you can concentration, dream, and let your inventiveness take off!

Design of the Fort: Arranging Your Work area

Plan your stronghold with care. A happy space is one that is free of clutter! Find the specialty of sorting out your work area, orchestrating your devices, and making a coding sanctuary that sparkles satisfaction and motivation.

Enrich with Enchantment: Tweaking Your Current circumstance

Add a dash of sorcery to your post! Customize your coding climate with tones, subjects, and perhaps a sprinkle of pixie dust. An agreeable and motivating space will make your coding undertakings much more magnificent.

Stronghold Safeguard: Supporting Your Spells Even the most powerful fort needs to be protected. Gain proficiency with the significance of sponsorship up your spells (code). We'll share straightforward stunts to guarantee your enchanted manifestations are completely safe, fit to be brought at whatever point required.

Prepare to release the sorcery inside your coding stronghold. The excursion has recently started, and your coding camp is currently prepared for the experiences that lie ahead!

3. Hi, World! Enchantment Spell

Ahoy, youthful alchemists! It's time to learn how to cast your first spell in Python, the enchanting programming language. As we invoke the timeless incantation, be prepared: Hi, World!"

3.1 Projecting Your Most memorable Spell: print("Hello, World!")

Get ready to cause the coding universe to hear your voice! In the hallowed looks of Python, the spell to welcome the world is basically as straightforward as articulating:

```python
Duplicate code
print("Hello, World!")
```

Release this sorcery in your coding wand (PC) and see as the words "Hi, World!" appear right in front of your eyes. It's not simply code; it's the most important phase in your excursion to ordering the magical powers of Python.

Direction for Beginner Spellcasters: Murmur to Your Wand: Open your code proofreader, type the spell precisely as displayed, and murmur it to your coding wand (execute the code).

Runes of Execution: Get familiar with the runes (console easy routes) to cause your wand to rejuvenate your spells. You'll be a Python guide in the blink of an eye!

Investigating Charms: In the event that the sorcery doesn't occur true to form, dread not! We'll investigate normal charms to investigate and troubleshoot your spells.

3.2 Figuring out the Enchanted behind the Spell

Now that you've projected the spell, how about we unwind the enchantment woven inside it. Python resembles a cordial genie; it pays attention to your orders and performs errands with an influx of your wand.

Translating the Spell:
print() Elixir: Grasp the print() mixture, a mysterious solution that makes your Python manifestations talk. We'll analyze its parts and perceive how it changes text into apparent miracles.

Citation Charm: The magical force of citations! Find the reason why words should be encased in statements, as we investigate the significance of correspondence in the coding domain.

Hi, World! Incantation: Dive into the significance of "Hi, World!" - the widespread hello that has started incalculable coding undertakings.

Plan to be entranced by the straightforwardness and force of your most memorable Python spell. You are now a budding wizard in the coding cosmos, and the journey has just begun!

4. Journey into Variables

ValleyWelcome to Variables Valley, a mystical realm where integers and strings are used to make potions. To unlock the mysteries of Python sorcery, you'll learn how to gather and mix these potions as you travel this magical landscape.

4.1 Buying Magical Remedies:

Strings and Integers In this section of our journey, let's investigate the two fundamental elixirs that Python provides: numbers and strings.

Gathering Numbers:
☐Whole numbers are the mixture of unadulterated mathematical sorcery. Perform basic arithmetic spells, learn to summon them into existence, and watch as numbers dance through your code.

python
Duplicate code

```
wizard_level = 42
elixir_quantity = 7
total_power = wizard_level + elixir_quantity
```

Gathering Strings:

The mystical incantations that bring text to life are strings. Find the specialty of creating words, sentences, and, surprisingly, secret messages in the language of Python.

python
Duplicate code

```
spell_book = "Python Mixtures"
welcoming = "Good tidings, supernatural coder!"
```

Go along with us as we leave on a journey to gather these otherworldly mixtures and use their powers to shape the coding scene.

4.2 Blending Mixtures: Variable Task Stunts

Now that we've assembled our mixtures, we should become familiar with the craft of elixir blending — allocating these mysterious elixirs to factors.

Doling out Elixirs:
The ancient method of giving your potions names makes them easier to conjure later. This is known as variable assignment. Disclose the privileged insights of the equivalent sign as you dole out mystical qualities to your factors.

python
Duplicate code
favorite_number = 7

mystical_word = "Abracadabra"
Fermenting Mixtures in Spells:
Put these tinctures together in your coding cauldron to make potent spells. Witness how factors can hold the substance of your mysterious manifestations and make your spells dynamic and versatile.

python
Duplicate code

```python
total_gold = wizard_level * 100
spell_result = mystical_word + " " + spell_book
```

Go along with us on this entrancing excursion as we navigate Factors Valley, gathering and blending mixtures to open the genuine capability of Python wizardry. Your coding experience has quite recently taken a mystical turn!

5. The Charmed Choice Woodland

Good tidings, daring swashbucklers! As you dive further into the mysterious grounds of Python, you'll end up in the Charmed Choice Woods. The trees here whisper secrets, and the powerful if statements direct you down a path that will take you on magical choices and daring adventures.

5.1 Exploring with if Explanations

The Charmed Choice Woodland is brimming with exciting bends in the road, and to explore this ethereal scene, you'll require the force of if articulations — the captivated compass of Python.

If Articulations:

Choice Trees: Learn how to create decision trees that use conditions to direct your code. In the event that a condition is met, an enchanted pathway opens before you.

```python
Duplicate code
wizard_level = 42


on the off chance that wizard_level >= 50:
    print("You have arrived at the most significant level of wizardry!")
else:
    print("Continue your mystical excursion, youthful understudy.")
```

☐☐Planning Your Way: Make a map of your route through the forest using if statements. Whether it's tracking down secret fortunes or keeping away from legendary animals, assuming that articulations are your aide.

Python's copy code for treasure_nearby returns true when treasure_nearby:

```
print("A money box glimmers somewhere out there. How will you respond?")
else:
print("The woodland is quiet. Continue to investigate.")
```

5.2 Simply deciding: Elif and Other Adventures:

As you travel through the forest, you'll come across situations in which a straightforward yes or no response is insufficient. Enter the domains of elif and else, where decisions become undertakings.

elif Experiences:

```
□else:
    print("You are in a magical space past entryways.")
else Experiences:
```

□□The Surprising Excursion: At the point when any remaining ways disappear, the else experience starts. Investigate the unforeseen, plan for shocks, and let your code answer the magical unexplored world.

```
python
Duplicate code
spell_cast = Bogus

in the event that spell_cast:
    print("The spell has been projected effectively.")
elif not spell_cast:
    print("The enchantment misfires away. Attempt another chant.")
```

```
else:
    print("You've entered a realm where magic has not existed.")
```

Step strongly through the Captivated Choice Timberland, where if proclamations, elif undertakings, and else shocks anticipate. Your Python process is turning out to be more charming with each code spell you cast!

6. Circling through the Time Travel

Welcome, people who jump through time! In the captivating place that is known for Python, time curves to the desire of circles. With the captivating For Loop and the mesmerizing While Loop, join us as we dance through the temporal tapestry and travel through the time warp.

6.1 Dance of the For Circle

Envision a dance floor where your code steps smoothly through a succession, rehashing moves like a very much arranged artful dance. Enter the scene, the For Circle — a dance accomplice that rehashes a bunch of directions a foreordained number of times.

For Circle Movement:

☐Dance of Cycle: Figure out how to skim through arrangements of numbers, components, or even supernatural antiques with the For Circle. Your code's rhythm is represented by a beat for each step of the loop.

python
Duplicate code

```
for step in range(5):
    print("Step", step + 1, ": Hit the dance floor with the enchanted wand!")
```

Range of Melody: Divulge the song of the reach() capability, your melodic sheet for the dance. The ethereal movements of your loop can be controlled in both tempo and direction.

Python Copy code for a beat in the range (1, 10, 2):

```
   print("Beat," ", "): Moving to the magical beat!")
```

6.2 Mission of the While Circle

As you venture further into the time travel, the scene changes, and the While Circle turns into your dependable aide. The While Loop dances as long as a particular condition holds true, in contrast to the For Loop.

While Circle Mission:

☐ Questing through Conditions: Leave on a mission through the time travel with the While Circle. It proceeds with the dance until a mysterious condition is not generally met.

python

Duplicate code
spell_power = 80

```
while spell_power > 0:
    print("Casting spell. Power that remains: spell_power)
    spell_power - = 10
```

☐ Limitless Conceivable outcomes: Not at all like the For Circle, the While Circle is unique. Make sure your quest has a way out so it doesn't get stuck in an infinite loop—great power comes with great responsibility!

Python's copy of the code with the mystical_portal_open = True condition while the portal is open:

```
    print("Stepping through the supernatural entrance!")
    mystical_portal_open = False #
```

Make sure the portal closes to avoid

endless adventures. Young travelers, dance through the time warp with the grace of the For Loop and the spirit of the questing that comes from the While Loop. Your Python process rises above time, and the circles are your associates in this hypnotizing experience!

7.Functions: Your Coding Spells Book

Welcome, youthful sorcerers! ◻✦ In the enchanted universe of Python, capabilities are your own personal spells — strong chants that permit you to make and project mysterious impacts. How about we jump into the otherworldly domain of capabilities and figure out how to characterize and project these coding spells freely.

7.1 Making Your Own Spells: Characterizing Capabilities

In the excellent library of Python, a capability resembles a spell that you can make and name, enabling you to play out a particular enchanted task at whatever point you call upon it. We should set out on an excursion to characterize your own personal spells!

Characterizing Spells:

python

Duplicate code

```python
def greet_wizard(name):

    "A spell to welcome wizards"

    print(f"Greetings, {name}! Welcome to the supernatural domain.")
```

Here, we've made a spell called out to greet_wizard that takes a wizard as a boundary and invites them to the supernatural domain. The triple-cited text is an enchanted depiction of your spell.

Utilizing Spells:

To project your recently characterized spell, just call out to its and give the fundamental fixings (contentions):

python

Duplicate code

```
greet_wizard("Merlin")
```

Watch in amazement as the spell springs to life, inviting the wizard Merlin to the enchanted place that is known for Python!

7.2 Projecting Spells Voluntarily: Calling Capabilities

Now that you've become amazing at spell creation, how about we investigate how to project these spells freely. Enchanting means summoning its power and seeing its otherworldly impacts.

Calling Spells:

python

Duplicate code

```python
def make_invisible(item):

    """A spell to make a thing invisible."""

    print(f"{item} has become imperceptible!")
```

Calling the spell to make an elixir undetectable

make_invisible("Magic Elixir")

With this spell, you can make any thing imperceptible just by calling the capability make_invisible and giving the thing as a fixing.

Captivating Groupings:

You can likewise utilize spells inside spells, making captivating groupings of sorcery:

python

Duplicate code

def perform_magic():

```python
    """A spell to play out a mystical sequence."""

    greet_wizard("Luna")

    make_invisible("Spell Book")


# Calling the spell to play out a supernatural grouping

perform_magic()
```

In this model, the perform_magic spell calls upon the recently characterized spells to welcome a wizard and make a spell book undetectable in a mysterious succession.

8. Lists: The Enchanted Assortment

Welcome, treasure trackers and antiquity finders! In the charming domain of Python, enter the area of Records — your otherworldly assortment where components join to make strong spells. Join us as we learn how to make lists, collect objects, and find hidden treasures.

8.1 Social event Antiques: Making Records

In the otherworldly universe of Python, a Rundown is an assortment of things that can be anything — mixtures, relics, or even bits of spells. We should plunge into the craft of social occasion antiques and making your own mysterious records.

Making Records:

Spell Books: Figure out how to wind around your own spell looks by making records. Every component in the rundown is a mysterious fixing, ready to be called.

python
Duplicate code

```python
spell_ingredients = ["Eye of Newt", "Phoenix Quill", "Mythical serpent Scale"]
```

☐ Blended Components: Embrace the flexibility of records. They can hold a blend of elixirs, numbers, or considerably different records. The sorcery is in your grasp!

```python
python Copy code mixed_elements = ["Magic Crystal", 42, "Invisibility Potion", "Levitation Charm"]]
```

8.2 Sorting and Looking for Treasure

Now that you have all of your magical items in your possession, it is time to set out on a journey through the List Kingdom. Find the craft of arranging, looking, and disclosing the fortunes inside.

Arranging Spells:

☐ In order Arranging: You can arrange your artifacts alphabetically by casting spells. Allow the wizardry to unfurl as the components orchestrate themselves in an agreeable grouping.

python
Duplicate code
```python
spell_ingredients.sort()
```

print("Sorted Spell Fixings:", spell_ingredients) Numbering: For records with mathematical curios, unwind the enchantment of mathematical arranging. Organize your fortunes from the littlest to the mightiest.

python
Duplicate code
```
treasure_values = [300, 50, 1000, 150]
treasure_values.sort()
print("Sorted Fortune Values:", treasure_values)
```
Looking for Fortune:
☐ Looking for the Captivated Thing: Use the force of ordering to uncover explicit curios in your mystical assortment. Each thing is a fortune ready to be found.

```python
Duplicate code
desired_item = "Phoenix Quill"
in the event that desired_item in spell_ingredients:
    print("You have seen as the sought after", desired_item + "!")
else:
    print(desired_item, "isn't in your assortment.")
```

Release the sorcery inside your Rundown Realm. Whether you're making records, arranging ancient rarities, or looking for treasures, the power is in your grasp. Your Python process is presently improved with the charm of records!

9. Dictionaries:

The Way to Hidden Treasures Greetings, mapmakers and treasure hunters! Enter the domain of Dictionaries, your ancient map that leads you to hidden treasures, in the magical world of Python. Go along with us as we leave on the specialty of guide making, opening insider facts, and getting to the mystical vaults inside.

9.1 Guide Making with Word references

In the tremendous scene of Python, a Word reference is your magical guide — an assortment of key-esteem coordinates that guides you to stowed away fortunes. How about we dig into the craft of guide making and make your own personal fortune map.

Making Guides:

☐☐Treasure Guide Creation: Gain proficiency with the specialty of making word references, where each key is an area, and each worth is the secret fortune. Release the force of the guide!

python
Duplicate code
```python
treasure_map = {
    "Woodland": " Brilliant Oak seeds",
    "Cave": " Precious stone Knife",
    "Knoll": " Mixed Treasures:
```
Sapphire Rose Explore the dictionaries' plethora of applications. Watch as your map transforms into a magical repository as you mix and match various treasures.

python
Duplicate code

```
mixed_treasures = {
    "Captivated Talisman": 150,
    "Antiquated Parchments": ["Levitation Spell", "Imperceptibility Potion"],
    "Secret Chamber": True
```

9.2 Gaining Access to Secrets: Getting to and Altering

Now that you've created your fortune map, now is the ideal time to open its insider facts. Find the magic of getting to and adjusting treasures inside the enchanted vaults.

Getting to Fortunes:

☐ ☐Utilizing Keys: Excel at utilizing keys to get to explicit fortunes. Each key is a mystery code that makes the way for a universe of mysterious conceivable outcomes.

python
Duplicate code

```
forest_treasure = treasure_map["Forest"]
print("Treasure in the Backwoods:", forest_treasure)
```

Access Conditional: Use conditional statements to access treasures only if certain conditions are met to safeguard your journey.

python
Duplicate code

```
desired_location = "Cavern"
if desired_location in treasure_map:
    print("You have arrived at the,", desired_location, and "). The fortune is", treasure_map[desired_location])
else:
```

```
    print("You are not where you
want to be.")
```

Altering Fortunes:

☐Refreshing the Guide: By updating your treasures, you can become the map's guardian. Adjust existing fortunes or add new ones to keep your guide current.

python
Duplicate code

```python
treasure_map["Meadow"]         =
"Emerald Bloom"
treasure_map["Riverbank"]       =
"Silver Fish"
print("Updated Fortune Guide:",
treasure_map)
```

☐☐ Monitoring Insider facts: Get familiar with the specialty of watching your fortunes. Utilize restrictive proclamations to alter cherishes just under specific mysterious conditions.

python
Duplicate code
```python
if treasure_map["Cave"] == "Gem Blade":
    treasure_map["Cave"] = "Gatekeeper Winged serpent"
    print("The treasure in the Cavern has changed into a Gatekeeper Winged serpent!")
```
Leave on your mission with the otherworldly guide of word references. Whether you're making maps, getting to treasures, or changing insider facts, the excursion will undoubtedly be loaded up with charm and revelation. Your Python experience presently embraces the wizardry of word references!

10. The Excellent Finale: Smaller than usual Python Tasks

Ok, dear wizards and sorceresses! As you approach the excellent finale of your Python experience, it's opportunity to exhibit your mystical ability through two captivating ventures. Prepare to plan your own personal Sorcery Mixture Blender and leave on an exhilarating excursion in the Winged serpent Tamer Game.

10.1 Planning Your Enchanted Elixir Blender

Envision yourself in an enchanted research facility encompassed by gurgling cauldrons and shining fixings. In this undertaking, you'll plan an Enchanted Mixture Blender where you can make and devise your own otherworldly elixirs.

Project Outline:

☐ Objective: Make a Python program that permits clients to blend different otherworldly fixings to create interesting elixirs.

Key Elements:

Fixing Determination: Give a rundown of supernatural fixings (e.g., Eye of Newt, Phoenix Plume, and so on.).

Client Association: Permit clients to pick fixings and amounts for their mixtures.

Blending Interaction: Carry out a capability that joins chosen fixings to make a supernatural mixture.

Display of Result: Exhibit the last mixture and its supernatural properties.

Model Code Piece:

python

Duplicate code

```
def mix_potion(ingredients):
    # Carry out the elixir blending rationale here
    # Return the last elixir

# Enchantment Elixir Blender
print("Welcome to the Enchanted Elixir Blender!")
ingredients_list = ["Eye of Newt", "Phoenix Quill", "Winged serpent Scale"]

# Client chooses fixings
selected_ingredients = ["Eye of Newt", "Mythical beast Scale"]

# Blend the mixture
result_potion = mix_potion(selected_ingredients)

# Show the outcome
```

```
print("Congratulations! A magical
potion has been made by you:
result_potion)
```

10.2 Structure Your Mythical serpent Tamer Game

Prepare yourselves, valiant globe-trotters, for the elating Winged serpent Tamer Game. In this undertaking, you'll leave on a mission to tame and cooperate with legendary winged serpents.

Project Outline:

☐ Objective: Foster a Python game where players can tame and collaborate with virtual mythical serpents.

Key Highlights:

Types of dragons: Make various sorts of mythical serpents with one of a kind qualities.

Subduing Component: Execute a subduing framework that expects clients to perform explicit activities to win the mythical beast's trust.

Connection Choices: Allow players to use user inputs to feed, play, or control their dragons.

Status: A dragon Show the ongoing status and temperament of the mythical serpent in light of connections.

Model Code Piece:

python

Duplicate code

```python
class Winged serpent:
    def __init__(self, name, type):
        self.name = name, self.type =
type, happiness = 50, and hunger =
30. Define feed(self):
        # Carry out taking care of
rationale
        self.happiness += 10
        self.hunger - = 15
```

```python
# Mythical serpent Tamer Game
print("Welcome to the Mythical serpent Tamer Game!")

# Make a mythical beast
player_dragon = Dragon("Ember", "Fire")

# Connect with the mythical beast
print(f"Meet {player_dragon.name}, your {player_dragon.type} mythical beast!")

# Feed the dragon with player_dragon.feed() # Show the dragon's status with print(f)"player_dragon.name"
```

"player_dragon.happiness" denotes happiness, and "player_dragon.hunger" denotes hunger.") Take on these magical endeavors, young wizards! Allow your imagination to take off as you plan an Elixir Blender and adventure into the universe of Mythical serpent Restraining. May your Python spells weave stories of charm and win in this great finale!

11. Observing Your Coding Triumph

Yahoo, otherworldly coders! ☐ You've effectively finished your Python experience and arisen as gifted magicians of the coding domain. Now is the right time to commend your accomplishments and loll in the greatness of your freshly discovered mysterious powers.

11.1 Your Python Experience Recognition

As a badge of acknowledgment for your commitment and dominance of Python spells, we present to you the esteemed Python Experience Recognition. This certificate ensures that you've vanquished the charmed terrains of Python, from the fundamentals of spells to the production of mystical undertakings.

Confirmation Subtleties:
Wizard Name: [Your Name]
Culmination Date: [Date of Completion]
Specialization: Python Magic
This certificate is a demonstration of your obligation to the coding create. Hang it gladly in your virtual wizard's lair!

11.2 Using Your Magical Skills Together: Coding Exhibit

Now that you've become amazing at Python divination, now is the right time to impart your mystical powers to the world. Consider sorting out a Coding Feature to display your captivated manifestations and move individual wizards-in-preparing.

Coding Grandstand Features:
Sorcery Elixir Blender Demo: Present your Enchanted Elixir Blender project. Show how various mixes of fixings lead to novel mixtures.

Mythical beast Tamer Game Grandstand: Welcome individual coders to connect with your Mythical beast Tamer Game. Allow them to observe the appeal and character of your virtual mythical serpents.

Code Walkthroughs: Share scraps of your #1 spells and make sense of the enchanted behind them. Feature any inventive methodologies or exceptional coding procedures you utilized.

Supernatural Minutes: Remember the mystical snapshots of your Python experience. Share accounts, challenges survive, and the delight of seeing your code become completely awake.

Rouse Others: Urge your kindred wizards to set out on their coding processes. Share your experiences, knowledge, and resources with others.

Festivity Party:
With your fellow coders, throw a virtual party to celebrate. Share stories, toast to your triumphs, and revel in the fellowship of the coding local area.

Congrats, powerful magicians! Your Python experience has been a victory, and the enchanted you've woven will keep on resounding in the coding universe. May your future coding missions be as charming and fulfilling!

12. Appendix: The Alchemist's Tool compartment

Welcome to the Alchemist's Tool compartment — a priceless asset for each wizard and sorceress exploring the supernatural terrains of Python. In this supplement, you'll find speedy reference spells and investigating charms to help you on your coding missions.

12.1 Spells for Quick Reference 1. Print Spell:

python
Duplicate code
print("Your mystical mantra here!")
Utilize this spell to cause your Python manifestations to talk and uncover their insider facts.

2. For Circle Mantra:
Python: Copy item in iterable code:

Your enchanted directions here
Conjure this spell to move through groupings of components in an elegant circle.

3. Word reference Creation:
python
Duplicate code

```python
my_dictionary = {
    "Key1": " Value1",
    "Key2": " Value2",
    # Add more mystical sections here
}
```

Make this spell to make your magical guides and open secret fortunes.

4. Creation of Functions:
python
Duplicate code

```python
def my_function(parameter1, parameter2):
```

```
   # Your otherworldly directions
here
   return magical_result
```
Ace this spell to make your own coding spells as capabilities.

5. List Conjuring:

Python's copy code for my_list = "Element1", "Element2," and "Element3"] Use this spell to collect magical artifacts and make lists of elements.

6. While Circle Appeal:

python
Duplicate code
```
while condition:
   # Your mystical directions here
```
Project this appeal to set out on journeys through the time travel, it is as of now not consistent with rehash activities until a condition.

12.2 Investigating Your Coding Cauldron

1. Mistake Divination:

When confronted with mistakes, counsel the supernatural blunder messages that Python gives. They frequently include clues regarding the nature of the problem.

2. Spell Sentence structure Checking:

Make sure your spell incantations adhere to correct syntax by employing the SyntaxError charm. Python is specific about how spells are composed.

3. Wand Investigation:

On the off chance that your code doesn't create the normal outcomes, investigate your coding wand (PC) for any issues. Guarantee it's in great shape and appropriately associated with the mystical organization.

4. Elixir Troubleshooting:
Utilize the print() elixir decisively to assess the upsides of factors and grasp the progression of your code.

5. Library Parchment Survey:
Find additional spells and magical functions that may aid your quest by perusing the documentation and scrolls of Python libraries.

6. Wizard Committee:
Consult the wise Wizard Council (communities and coding forums). Individual wizards could give bits of knowledge and answers for your coding difficulties.

May these charms and spells help you through successes and

challenges in coding. The Alchemist's Tool stash is your confided in buddy, guaranteeing that your cauldron rises with effective charms!